This Is Sweden
A Kid's Guide To Stockholm, Sweden

Photography By John D. Weigand
Poetry By Penelope Dyan

Bellissima Publishing, LLC
Jamul, California
www.bellissimapublishing.com

copyright © 2011 by Penny D. Weigand and John D. Weigand

All rights reserved. No part of this book may be reproduced or transmitted in any form or by any means, electronic or mechanical, including photocopying, recording, or by any other means, or by any information or storage retrieval system, without permission from the publisher.

ISBN 978-1-61477-003-9

First Edition

For all of the Andersons, wherever you are!

This Is Sweden
Bellissima Publishing, LLC

Introduction

The city of Stockholm is over 700 years old and it spreads across 14 islands, facing out to the Baltic Sea. You can get to just about all of Stockholm's sites on foot, as did our photographer and author; and this is a great way to see Stockholm! You can also take a boat trip that will give you a different facet of Scandinavia's largest and probably most beautiful city. Stockholm is a great family place to visit with loads of things to see, and lots of fun stuff for kids to do!

Take an imaginary journey through the pages of this book and make it your own by adding pictures, postcards, tickets and notes to this book as you go along on your visit with award winning author, attorney and former teacher, Penelope Dyan and our photographer, John D. Weigand.

To travel is to create a memory and a dream all of your very own. Take the time to savor and enjoy the feel and warmth of this beautiful city.

This Is Sweden
Bellissima Publishing, LLC

This Is Sweden
A Kid's Guide To Stockholm, Sweden

Photography By John D. Weigand
Poetry By Penelope Dyan

The brightly colored train station
stands illuminated in the morning sun.
The trip to Stockholm has just begun.
You'll get your tickets for the train.
Sadly, they've predicted rain.
If it doesn't rain, you are told,
it will probably be very cold.
Still to Stockholm you will go,
happy that there is NO snow!

You get into stockholm and you look
for something sweet.
The small brown cobblestones
are wet beneath your feet.

Bicycles line a tunnel leading
to some little shops.
There is a constant light rain now,
that just will NOT stop.
You cannot find an umbrella to buy.
It doesn't matter HOW hard you try!
So you duck into this tunnel instead
keeping raindrops off of your head!

Near the palace you see two horses.
One looks big.
The other (far away) looks small.
But both are on pedestals.
They are full sized, and quite tall!

You keep on walking.
You see THIS beautiful sight.
Mom says you'll take a river cruise
before it turns night.

You take pictures and some notes, when you see these sailboats.

There is a beautiful building.
Boats line up below.
You wonder where it is
that these sailboats will go.

At the Vasa Warship Museum
you go inside,
and from THIS ship you cannot hide.
Sunk in 1628, toppled by winds,
because of too many heavy arms,
now recovered from the seas
it has not lost its charms.
You have NEVER seen ANYTHING
quite like THIS before.
You can almost hear its cannons roar!

The ship stands against the light.
It is a beautiful and ominous sight.
It seems it was the powers that be,
left it preserved beneath the sea.

And in a ship's nest
you can stop and play.
This has turned out to be
a very fun day!

Here is something else to do before it gets dark.
You can go and have fun in this amusement park!

From the river boat
you can see this crane giraffe!
You look at your mother
and you start to laugh.
And finally there is no more rain,
As you hop aboard
the click-clackity train.
And as you travel down the track,
you know someday
that you'll come back.
It doesn't matter
WHERE you begin or start. . .

> "WHEREVER YOU GO, GO WITH ALL YOUR HEART."
>
> — CONFUCIUS

www.ingramcontent.com/pod-product-compliance
Ingram Content Group UK Ltd.
Pitfield, Milton Keynes, MK11 3LW, UK
UKHW060135240426
12048UKWH00002B/47